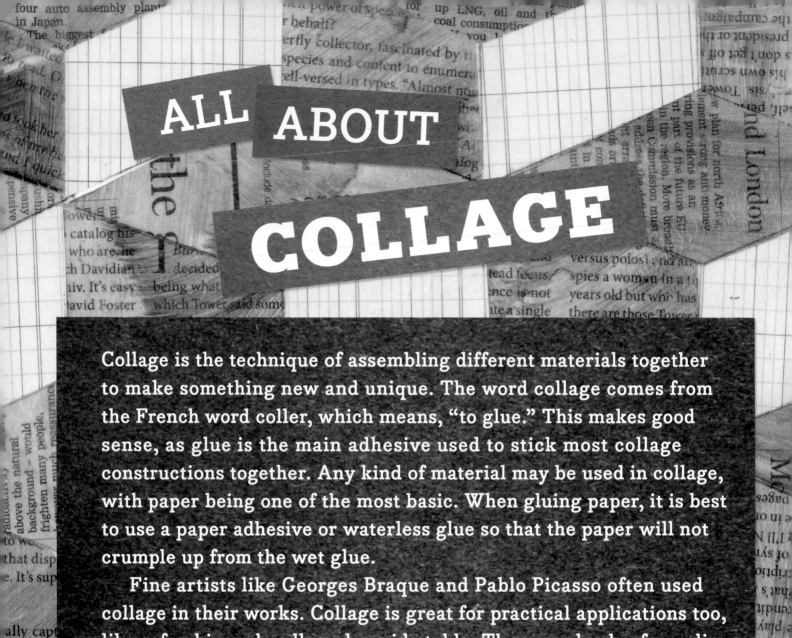

ALL ABOUT
the
COLLAGE

Collage is the technique of assembling different materials together to make something new and unique. The word collage comes from the French word coller, which means, "to glue." This makes good sense, as glue is the main adhesive used to stick most collage constructions together. Any kind of material may be used in collage, with paper being one of the most basic. When gluing paper, it is best to use a paper adhesive or waterless glue so that the paper will not crumple up from the wet glue.

Fine artists like Georges Braque and Pablo Picasso often used collage in their works. Collage is great for practical applications too, like refreshing a headboard or side table. There are loads of supplies lying around the house that are perfect collage materials, like old magazines and newspapers. If you are working with family photos or anything special, make a copy and use the duplicate for your collage. From wallpaper to fine art, the possibilities with collage are seemingly endless!

TODD OLDHAM

Designed, written and photographed by Todd Oldham Studio:
Yoshi Funatani, Greg Kozatek, Tony Longoria, Hillary Moore & Jennifer Whitney
Models: Azra, Miranda, Saevar & Samir
Library of Congress: 2012930846 ISBN: 9781934429891

AMMO
AMERICAN MODERN BOOKS

SUPPLY IDEAS

Just about any material can be used in collage! There are lots of free materials like paper scraps, old boxes, magazines, and fabric scraps that work perfectly for collage. Stickers and tapes work well as they function both as adhesive and art. Paint mixes well with collage and can be used in tinting paper or preparing a background. You can collage on just about anything with the proper glue. Decoupage glue is ideal for collage with the extra advantage of being both the glue and the sealer.

POST MODERN POST CARD

make your own post cards by sealing your collage under strips of clear packing tape

YOU WILL NEED
clear packing tape, white glue, scissors, and lots of found materials

1

Write your message, return address, and send-to address on a piece of paper.

2

Lay out several stripes of tape, sticky side up, overlapping the edges ¼ inch to create the front of your card. Repeat steps for the back of the card.

3

Place your message and addresses face down on the tape.

4

Cut, collage, and place the papers facing both down and up as you wish to create your artwork.

5

To finish, add more strips of clear tape to the sticky side of the card, carefully smoothing it down to avoid bubbles. Trim off the edges and apply a stamp to mail.

DYNAMIC DECOUPAGE

old newspaper and paint can dynamically dress up any surface

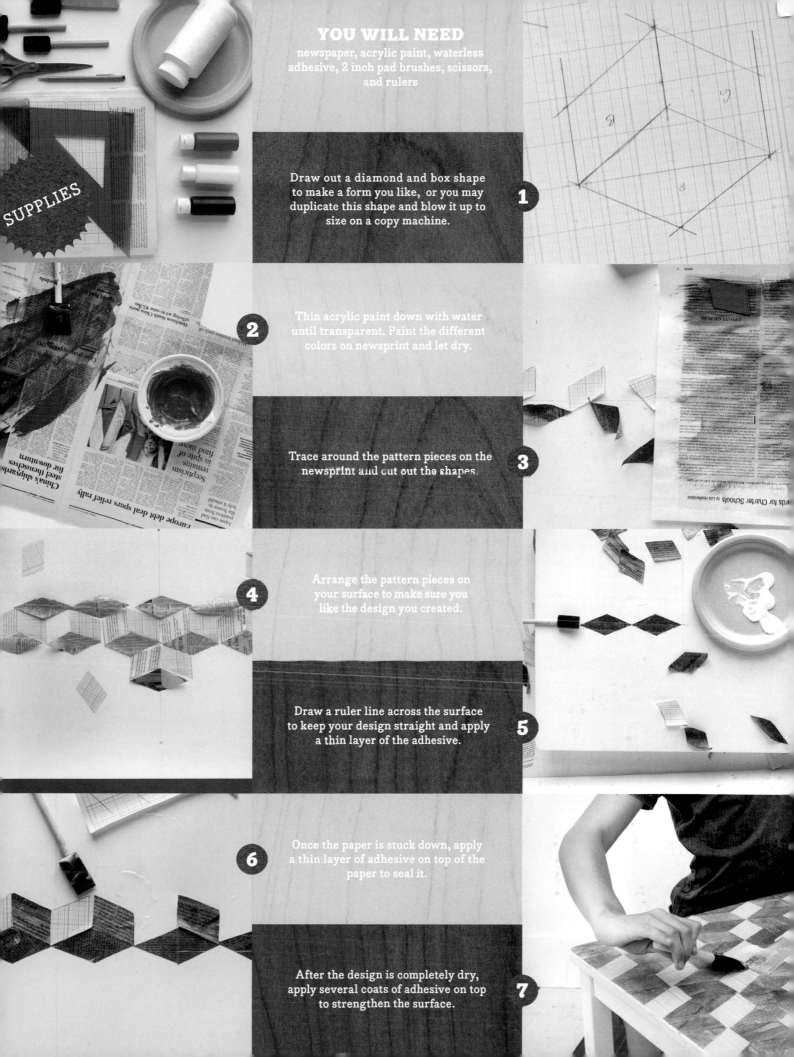

YOU WILL NEED

newspaper, acrylic paint, waterless adhesive, 2 inch pad brushes, scissors, and rulers

SUPPLIES

1 Draw out a diamond and box shape to make a form you like, or you may duplicate this shape and blow it up to size on a copy machine.

2 Thin acrylic paint down with water until transparent. Paint the different colors on newsprint and let dry.

3 Trace around the pattern pieces on the newsprint and cut out the shapes.

4 Arrange the pattern pieces on your surface to make sure you like the design you created.

5 Draw a ruler line across the surface to keep your design straight and apply a thin layer of the adhesive.

6 Once the paper is stuck down, apply a thin layer of adhesive on top of the paper to seal it.

7 After the design is completely dry, apply several coats of adhesive on top to strengthen the surface.

PRETTY IN PAPER

collage this festive frock made from all kinds of papers

YOU WILL NEED
scissors, paper towels, old magazines,
computer print-outs or anything else
you love, decorative tape, a stapler,
waterless adhesive

Fold a large envelope in half and draw a tank
top shape on it, or tape down the shape along
the side, neck, and armhole. Use additional
envelopes for larger sizes. Cut out and tape
the sides and shoulders together. Cut up the
center back to make it easy to wear.

1

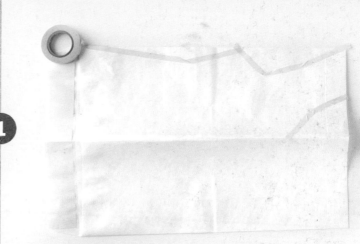

2

Pleat a handful of paper towels
to make the skirt.

Staple the pleated paper panels around
the bottom and tape over the staples so
they won't scratch.

3

4 Collage magazine cutouts around the dress by painting waterless adhesive on the top and bottom of the cutouts.

Finish applying the cutouts and let dry.

5

6 Pleat crepe paper and glue down between the top and the skirt of the dress.

Staple pleated circles of crepe paper into dots.

7

8 Apply the dots using glue.

9 Glue center decorations of contrasting paper in the center of the dots.

10 Trim off any excess paper and apply the remaining decorative tape.

11 Use tape to secure your finished dress. Close in the back and enjoy.

PAPER PATTERN POP

make instant pleated pop art

14

YOU WILL NEED
bright solid papers for the background and
printed papers for the face, tape or staplers

1

Pleat the paper used on the front of your
collage like a fan. Run your fingernail
down the pleats for a sharp edge. Carefully
make cuts along one side of the folds,
making sure not to cut through to the
opposite side.

2

Repeat cutting on the opposite fold side.

3

Open up your pleated paper and lay it on top
of the background paper and trim to size.
Staple or tape the two papers together and
hang up your new art!

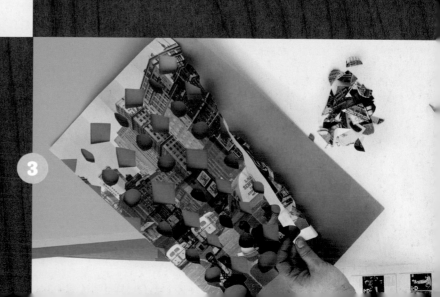

CUBED COLLAGE

create custom stackable blocks using a wide array of materials

YOU WILL NEED
wooden blocks, a collection of patterned magazine cutouts, tissue papers, recycled packaging, waterless glue, pencil, scissors

1

Draw around a cube to make a pattern and cut out.

2

Trace the pattern onto the paper you want to collage. Apply a thin layer of adhesive to the wooden block and stick the paper down in line with the edges.

3

Apply a thin layer of adhesive on top of the paper to seal it to the block.

4

You can collage first and trim later by painting a thin layer of adhesive to the block and then laying the paper on top.

5

When dry, trim off the excess paper and seal with a thin layer of adhesive.

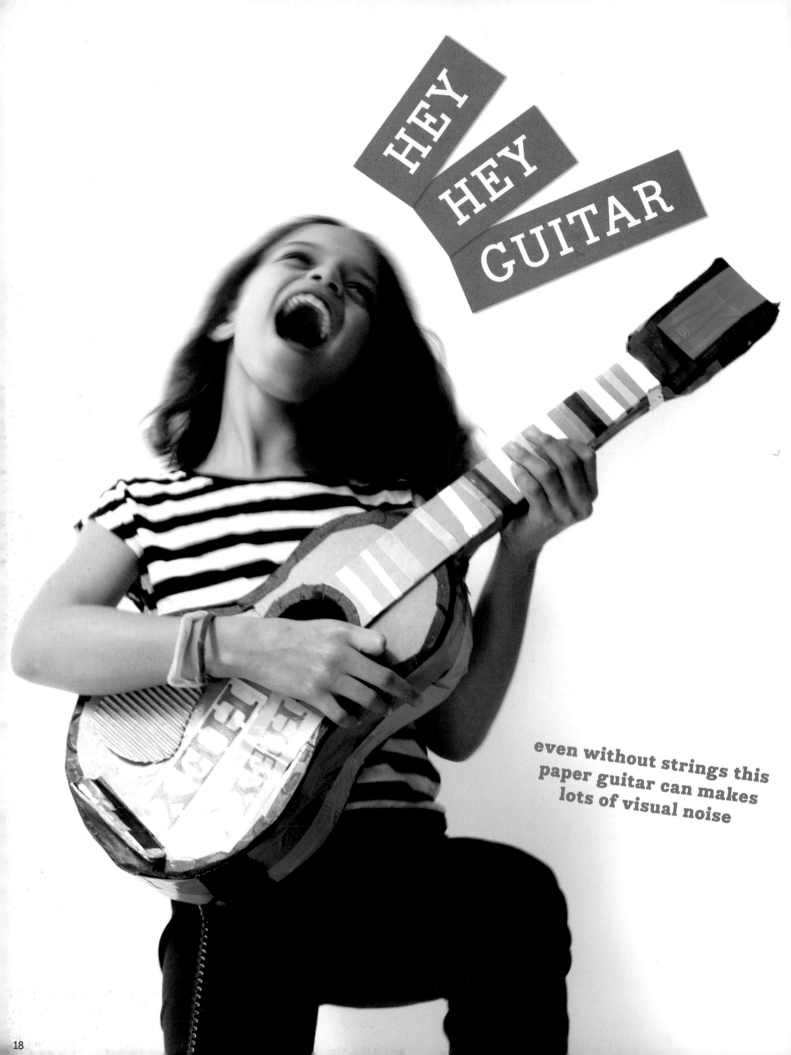

HEY HEY GUITAR

even without strings this paper guitar can makes lots of visual noise

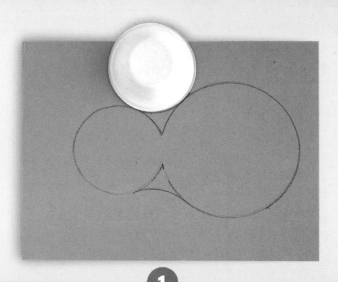

YOU WILL NEED

cardboard or very heavyweight paper, assorted tapes, glue, scissors, foam brush, decorative papers

1

Draw the body of the guitar using a large and small bowl or plates, as shown. Connect the space between the two circles with a curved line.

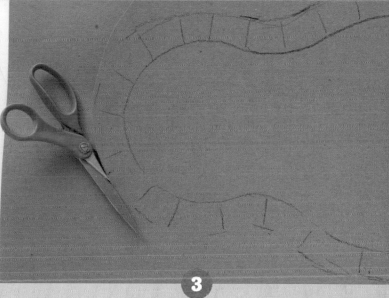

2

Trace around the shape and add a 2 inch border around the shape.

3

Cut out the shape and make slits around the edge, about every 2 inches.

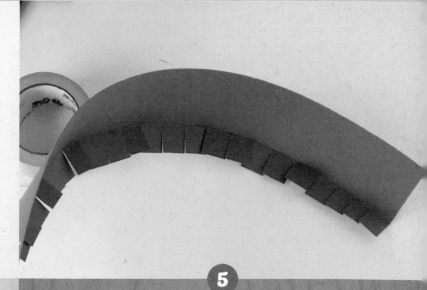

4

Bend the cut edge upward to create a place to attach the sides of the guitar.

5

Measure around the body shape and cut a piece of cardboard 5 inches wide by the measured length. Cut slits every 2 inches along one side that are 1 inch deep.

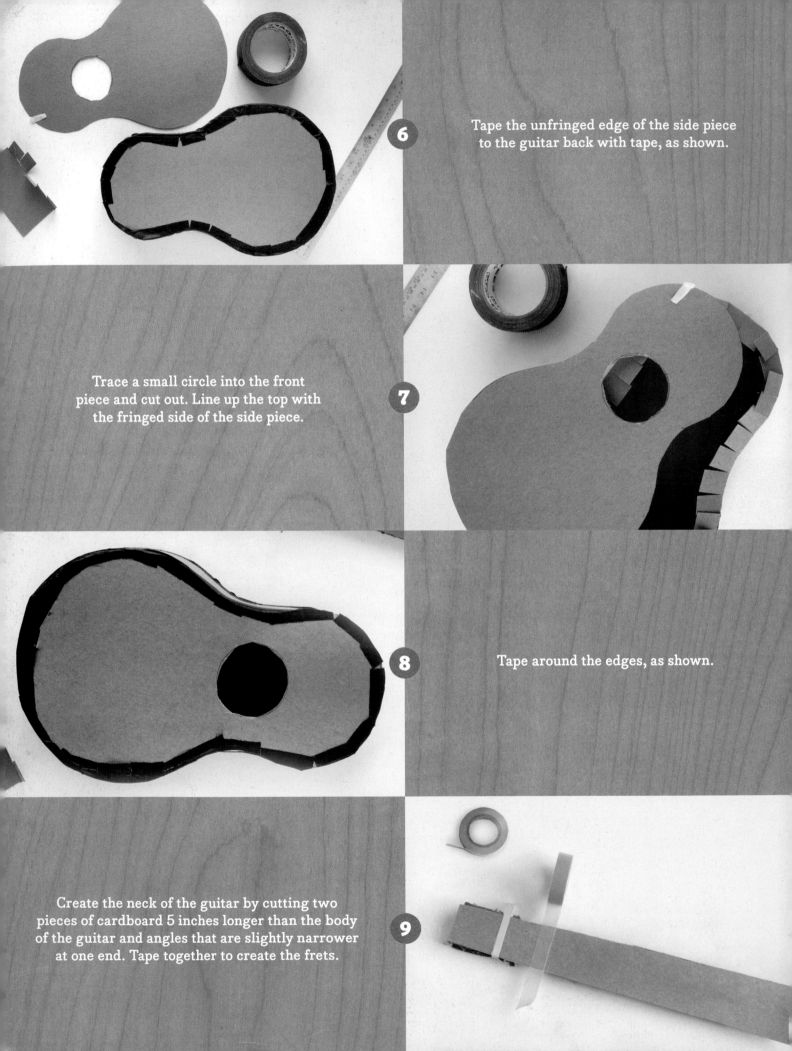

6 Tape the unfringed edge of the side piece to the guitar back with tape, as shown.

Trace a small circle into the front piece and cut out. Line up the top with the fringed side of the side piece.

7

8 Tape around the edges, as shown.

Create the neck of the guitar by cutting two pieces of cardboard 5 inches longer than the body of the guitar and angles that are slightly narrower at one end. Tape together to create the frets.

9

10 Trim off the backside of the neck while lining up the front to the center hole, and glue down. Add a piece of cardboard to create the head piece so that it's a little wider than the neck and about 6 inches long.

Add tape on the back of the neck after you have completed the decoration on the front side for a clean look.

11

12 Add tape to decorate the sides and back for added elements.

Add any additional decorative elements, including rubber band strings, or tape your mp3 player to the inside for the DIY air guitar experience!

13

FANTASTIC FAMILY PORTRAITS

collage a new look for your family portraits

YOU WILL NEED
masonite panel or stretched canvas, waterless adhesive, sponge brush, magazine cutouts, photocopied family pictures

1

Cut out your family pictures and any additional imagery to collage with.

2

Apply a thin layer of the adhesive to the canvas.

3

Place the first layer of images down onto the canvas and apply more adhesive on top.

4

Trim up any additional images to fit the collage as you like and glue them down.

5

Let dry completely and apply a final layer of the adhesive to secure your new work. Now organize an art show for your friends!

BOOM
DECK

custom skateboard
design inspired by old
school boomboxes

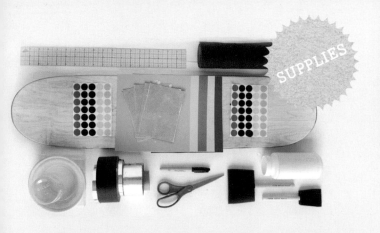

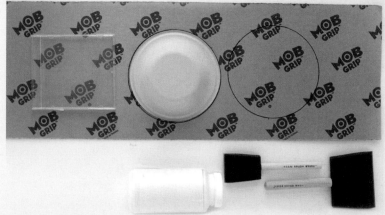

YOU WILL NEED
deck, assorted stickers and papers, waterless adhesive, sponge brush, paper bowl, scissors

1

Use a bowl to trace around to make speaker circles and cut out.

2

Use bottles or jar lids to trace additional circles and cut out.

3

Apply a thin layer of adhesive to the deck and stick down the first cutouts.

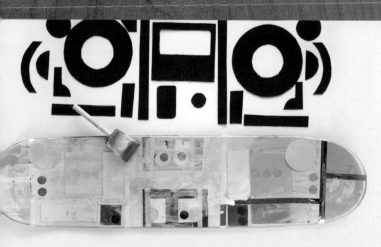

4

Apply another thin layer and arrange the top layer of cutouts, then place on deck.

5

Add a final coat of adhesive to the deck. Let it dry before it is street ready.

IRON ON GRAFFITI

there are other fun ways to
use iron-on repair fabrics

YOU WILL NEED

Iron [ask a grown-up to help with the ironing], scissors, washed t-shirt, assorted iron-on fabric pieces

1. Draw out the shapes you wish to use in your design.

2. Carefully cut them out.

3. Place them down on the t-shirt to create your design.

4. Iron on the pieces using the technique suggested on the iron-on piece instructions.

SUPPLIES

1

2

3

4

TISSUE PAPER PLANETS

tissue paper is a classic supply for collage, but this project is out of this world